Steamy

COUPONS

SOURCEBOOKS CASABLANCA™
AN IMPRINT OF SOURCEBOOKS, INC.®
NAPERVILLE, ILLINOIS

Published by Sourcebooks, Inc.
P.O. Box 4410, Naperville, Illinois 60567-4410
(630) 961-3900
FAX: (630) 961-2168
www.sourcebooks.com

ISBN 1-57071-886-5

Printed and bound in the United States of America
DR 10 9 8 7 6 5 4 3 2

Here are forty-four coupons to
tempt, tease, and *tantalize* your lover.
They work every time…

Steamy

With this coupon,
I'll kiss every inch of you,
from the top of your head
to the tips of your toes.

Steamy

This coupon entitles you to
one game of *strip poker*.

Steamy

This coupon entitles you to the longest, deepest *French kiss* you've ever had.

Steamy

With this coupon, you get to
kiss me from the top of
my head to the tips of my toes.

Steamy

With this coupon,
we'll do it *outside*.

Steamy

With this coupon,
I'll *feed you* aphrodisiacs
and satisfy your every desire.

Steamy

Want to *see a little* strip tease?
Just present this coupon.

Steamy

With this coupon,
I'll *whisper* in your ear
until your soul is on fire.

Steamy

When you present this coupon before
we go out, I'll go sans *panties*
for the whole evening.

Steamy

With this coupon, I will kiss you
wherever you want me to,
until you *tell me* to stop.

Steamy

With this coupon, you will get a sexy note from me every day for a week, and then I'm going to *pounce*!

Steamy

Present this coupon and I'll provide
the *champagne* and sexy videos.

Steamy

Present this coupon
for a long, *luxurious*, hot bath
followed by wanton behavior.

Steamy

With this coupon,
I will *nibble*, lick, and
kiss every inch of you.

Steamy

With this coupon,
I'll *act out* your
deepest, darkest fantasy.

Steamy

With this coupon,
you can *talk dirty* to me.

Steamy

With this coupon, I'll take you
to a secret *love nest*
for a weekend of bliss.

Steamy

When you present this coupon,
I'll meet you on my *lunch break*
for an hour of hot sex.

Steamy

This coupon entitles you to a full day
of both of us doing everything
in the *nude* (at home, of course!).

Steamy

With this coupon, I'll provide you with
a full bottle of *whipped cream*
to do with whatever you wish!

Steamy

With this coupon,
you can lick *honey* off
whatever part of me you wish.

Steamy

With this coupon,
let's do it in the *backseat*.

Steamy

This coupon entitles you to take me to the *movies*, where we'll sit in the back row and kiss the whole time.

Steamy

With this coupon, let's go shopping
for *lingerie* to be modeled
when we get home.

Steamy

This coupon is good for one lovemaking session in the *morning* before work.

Steamy

When you present this coupon,
we're off to an island for a
weekend of *tropical* bliss.

Steamy

With this coupon, I'll wear all *leather*.

Steamy

With this coupon,
new sexy *underwear* for both of us.

Steamy

With this coupon,
I'll brush your entire body
with a *feather* duster.

Steamy

With this coupon,
I'll *tickle* your most sensitive spot
with a feather.

Steamy

With this coupon, I'll cover both our *bodies* in sensual massage oil, then roll around with you.

Steamy

With this coupon,
I'll eat *dessert* off your belly.

Steamy

When you present this coupon,
we'll make love once in
every room of the house
over the next week.

Steamy

With this coupon, I'll go with you
wherever you want to go
and do *whatever you want* to do
once we get there.

Steamy

This coupon is good for one modeling session in bustierre, garters, and stiletto *heels*.

Steamy

With this coupon, I'll meet you at your office wearing *nothing* under my raincoat—you call the shots from there.

Steamy

This coupon is good for a session of belly dancing with *seven veils* and exotic music and foods.

Steamy

With this coupon,
you get to be my *love slave* for a day,
and I will have my way with you.

Steamy

With this coupon, I will lay you back
luxuriously among many *pillows*,
feed you grapes one by one,
and grant your every desire.

Steamy

Wherever we are when you present this coupon, I will tickle the back of your *neck*.

Steamy

With this coupon, be careful
what you ask for, *you just might* get it.

Steamy

With this coupon, we'll get *wet*—
in a hot tub, in a pool, in the rain,
on a waterbed—you name it.

Steamy

With this coupon,
we'll make love on a rug
in front of a blazing *fire*.

Steamy

With this coupon,
I'll meet you in the *backyard*—
you bring the champagne,
I'll bring the candle and the blanket.

Steamy

With this coupon, I'll

_____

_____

_____

Steamy

With this coupon, you

_____

_____

_____

Steamy